American History Time Lines

Big • Reproducible • Easy-to-Use

By Susan Washburn Buckley

SCHOLASTIC
PROFESSIONAL BOOKS

New York • Toronto • London • Auckland • Sydney

For Lora French, who first taught me how to find out what I want to know.

Cover design by Vincent Ceci and Jaime Lucero
Interior design by Drew Hires
Interior illustrations by Drew Hires
Photo research by Laura A. Kreiss

Cover photos: Benjamin Franklin: AP/Wide World Photos; Ship: Leonard Weisbard/Plymouth;
Statue of Liberty: Richard Laird/FPG International; Lunar Rover: NASA; Electrical Machine: The Franklin Institute;
Frederick Douglass: Library of Congress.

Interior photos: Pages 44 (bottom right), 45 (bottom right), 46, 76, 77, 78, 79, 80, 81, and 82: NASA;
all other photos courtesy of the Library of Congress.

ISBN 0-590-26608-X

Table of Contents

Introduction

12 Great Ways to Use These Time Lines!

1. Bulletin Board and Wall Displays

Reproduce the sheets of each time line on sturdy paper. (Try using different colored papers to distinguish time periods—say, a different color for each 100-year segment.)

To assemble the time lines, cut off the right hand margin along the vertical dotted lines, then overlap the sheets aligning with the dotted line at the left side (see the diagram below); then paste or tape the sheets together to assemble the full time line.

Display the time lines at students' eye level on classroom walls or bulletin boards.

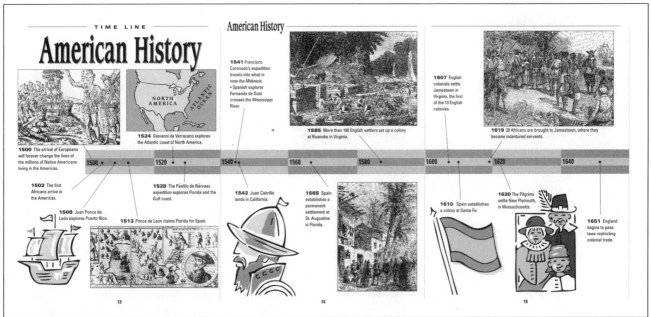

2. Make a Mini Time Line

Encourage students to make their own mini time lines on people or events that interest them. Each mini time line should be written on one sheet of paper. (Drawings are nice, too!)

Post the mini time lines above or below the main time line. Use yarn or string to relate the mini time line to the appropriate date.

3. Make Connections

As students use the time lines with their study of American history, they will begin to make connections between one event and another. When you work with a time line like *Growth of the Nation*, help students link events—for example, the arrival of the first printing press and the publication of the first American books.

Place a supply of string or different colored yarns near the time line. Suggest that students link related events, explaining each link on an index card above or below the time line. Or, they can make a link and ask other students to guess the connection.

Or, give students colored stars or circles they can paste next to related dates on the time line—for example, all of the events leading up to the American Revolution or all of the entries related to baseball.

4. Find Out More

Each day invite one student or cooperative group to choose something that especially interests them on a time line.

Ask the researchers to find out more about their subject and report to the class.

5. Map It

Make your time lines geographical. Have students draw or photocopy maps of places where time line events take place.

Post the maps near the related dates and use yarn or string to link them.

6. Date That Name

"People" your time lines by adding names and birth dates to them. As students meet the people of American history, have them add their names to the time lines.

Use sticky notes or index cards to record the person's name, important dates, and interesting information.

Place the sticky note or card on the time line or link it to a time line date with yarn or string.

7. Who/Where/When Am I?

Set up games for students to play using the time lines. Twenty Questions would be a good one. Students can investigate more about a person or event on a time line, then ask the class to play Twenty Questions to guess who their subject is, where the subject lived or where an event took place, and so on.

8. "TouchyFeely" Time Lines

Imaginative students can make sensory time lines by enhancing entries on one of the time lines provided.

With some research students can find out more about what people ate at a particular time, what they might have seen and heard, what clothes they wore, what music they heard.

Students can decorate the time line with drawings, cutout pictures, song lyrics, descriptions of smells, sights, sounds—even swatches of material, dried flowers, buttons, or the like.

9. Sticky Dates

All of these time lines will be better if students interact with them. Encourage students to add information to the time lines based on their reading and your class study of American history.

Place a supply of sticky notes near the time line so that students can add entries—or supplement existing entries—on their own.

Remind students of the importance of recording their information accurately. Suggest that they double check all dates and spelling to be sure they are correct before posting the information on the time line.

10. Parallel Bars

More advanced students can create parallel, or multiple strand, time lines using several of the time lines in this book.

Post the *Growth of the Nation* time line. Then duplicate one of the specialized time lines— *American Women*, for example—on paper of a different color. Place the sheets of the second time line underneath sheets of the same dates on the larger time line.

Ask students to draw inferences about relationships between events on the two time lines.

11. History Mysteries

Each 25-year segment of the *Growth of the Nation* time line contains one History Mystery for students to solve. Assign students or ask for volunteers to answer each question. The answers are as follows:

History Mystery Answers

1624—Cows were brought from England. 1638—Swedish settlers in Delaware. 1673—Regular horseback mail service begins between New York and Boston. 1699—Pirate William Kidd visited a friend in Narragansett, Rhode Island, and left some treasure there. 1706—Benjamin Franklin. 1732—George Washington. 1752—Ben Franklin found electricity in lightning with a kite and a key. 1777—Congress designated the Stars and Stripes as the official U.S. flag. 1814—The Star Spangled Banner. 1844—Inventor Morse sent the first telegraph message, "What hath God wrought." 1859—The first producing oil well. 1876—The United States celebrates its first centennial. 1909—The North Pole. 1927—Pilot Charles Lindbergh flew the first nonstop solo flight across the Atlantic. 1962—John Glenn in *Friendship 7.* 1976—Our bicentennial, or 200th birthday.

12. Book o' Time

Some students may want to start their own American history reference books or fact files. Duplicate the sheets of the time lines on three-hole-punch paper so that students can keep them in special notebooks. Encourage students to add their own specialized time lines to their notebooks.

Kids in History

This special time line is designed to give kids a chance to create their own unique time line. Invite students to research the events on the time line so they can add to it by drawing pictures or attaching copies of photos they've found in books or cut out from newspapers and magazines set aside for this purpose. Encourage them to make graphs, charts, and maps to attach to the time line. They also may want to add three-dimensional items, such as small toys, where appropriate. Some students may enjoy interviewing their parents and grandparents about some of the more recent events. Have them write up their interviews and attach them to the time line near the events they describe.

5 Ways to Teach Kids About Time

1. Walking Time

When your entire life has lasted only 10 or 12 years, it is almost impossible to grasp the concept of a century, to say nothing of a millennium. Imagining increments of time as physical or tangible units can help children understand the measurement of time.

On the playground or in a gym ask children to pace out a number of steps to match their age. Mark the beginning point and each year on the ground with chalk.

Position a student at the beginning point—call it "today"—and then ask a student to pace out 10 years and stop, imagining that they are going back in time. Have a succession of students pace from "today" back 20 years, 30 years, and so on until you have marked a century.

Ask students to imagine how long their line would be and how many students it would take to go back 1000 years.

2. Flying Time

You can use a kite and a kite string to show children time distances in a different way. Outside, on a good windy day, ask children to imagine that each time you unroll the kite string one year is passing. How far away is the kite in 100 years? Speculate with children about what you will be doing as each year passes.

Or, reverse the process and imagine that each turn takes you back in time one year. Have some significant dates in mind to give students to tell them what happened 10 years ago, 25 years ago, and so on.

3. Folding/Rolling Time Lines

You can make your own time lines using perforated computer paper or calculator tape. For example, using perforated computer paper you can give students a dramatic timetable of the history of the Americas. Have a connected set of paper at least 120 sheets long. Tell students that each sheet of paper stands for 100 years. Holding the end sheet, which represents today, unfold the paper sheet by sheet. The first sheet is the 1900s, the second is the 1800s. When you unfold the third sheet—the 1700s—say that the Declaration of Independence was signed and the Revolution was fought on this sheet. When you unfold the fourth sheet—the 1600s—point out that the first English colonies were founded at the beginning of this sheet. Tell students on the fifth sheet—the 1500s—that Spanish explorers were in the Americas. And on the sixth sheet—the 1400s—have students tell you what happened at the end of the sheet (Columbus landed in the Americas.)

At this point show students the remaining stack of sheets and tell them that for all of this time Native Americans were living in the Americas, before other people arrived. Explain that we don't know exactly when the first people arrived in this hemisphere—some scholars believe it was as long as 40,000 years ago. But scientists have proof that people were here about 12,000 years ago.

You can do the same thing by measuring off lengths of calculator tape or a long piece of string.

4. Clothesline Time Lines

Joy Hakim, author of the excellent series *A History of US,* loves time lines. She suggests stringing a clothesline around the walls of the classroom. For an American history time line, mark off time segments starting with 1400 or 1600, up to 2000. (You might want to leave a length of line hanging before the first date, to show that there was American history before the Europeans arrived!) Keep a supply of clothespins handy so that throughout the year students can hang up pictures, artifacts, and information cards at appropriate dates on this interactive time line.

5. Talking Time Lines

Often it is hard for children to realize that the words and dates on a time line represent real events in real people's lives. To help children see the humanity in history, writer Christina Cocek developed "talking time lines." To create a talking time line, a group of students should research one time period—the years leading up to the American Revolution, for example. Each student in the group might choose to be one person associated with the period. Students should select important dates associated with their character. Arranging themselves in the order of those dates, the students perform as a "talking time line." In a "talking time line" on the Road to Revolution, one student might begin by saying "The year is 1754. I am George Washington. I have just led my troops in the first fight of the French and Indian War. Our victory is part of a chain of events that will lead to revolution."

In another version, each student can represent an event. As students describe their events in order, they present a living chronology. "I am the French and Indian War..." "I am the Stamp Act..." and so on.

> *"Time is a sort of river of passing events, and strong is its current; no sooner is a thing brought to sight than it is swept by and another takes its place,..."*
> Marcus Aurelius

Resources

These books—sources of the information in these time lines—are useful resources for teachers and students.

Carruth, Gorton. *The Encyclopedia of American Facts and Dates*. HarperCollins Publishers, New York, 1993.

Daniel, Clifton (Editorial Director). *Chronicle of America*. Chronicle Publications, Mount Kisco, NY, 1989.

Dictionary of American Biography. Scribner, New York, 1946, 1964.

Estell, Kenneth (Editor). *The African-American Almanac, 6th Edition*. Detroit: Gale Research, Inc., 1994.

Grun, Bernard. *The Timetables of History*. Simon & Schuster, New York, 1991.

Porter, Kirk H. *A History of Suffrage in the United States*. University of Chicago Press, Chicago, 1918.

Trager, James. *The Women's Chronology*. Henry Holt and Company, New York, 1994.

American History

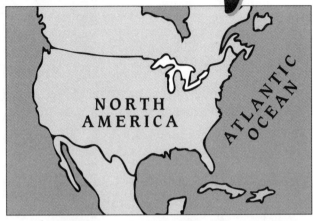

1524 Giovanni da Verrazano explores the Atlantic coast of North America.

1500 The arrival of Europeans will forever change the lives of the millions of Native Americans living in the Americas.

1500 • • • 1520 • •

1502 The first Africans arrive in the Americas.

1528 The Pánfilo de Nárvaez expedition explores Florida and the Gulf coast.

1508 Juan Ponce de León explores Puerto Rico.

1513 Ponce de León claims Florida for Spain.

American History

1541 Francisco Coronado's expedition travels into what is now the Midwest.
• Spanish explorer Fernando de Soto crosses the Mississippi River.

1585 More than 100 English settlers set up a colony at Roanoke in Virginia.

1540 ••	1560 •	1580 •

1542 Juan Cabrillo lands in California.

1565 Spain establishes a permanent settlement at St. Augustine in Florida.

1607 English colonists settle Jamestown in Virginia, the first of the 13 English colonies.

1619 20 Africans are brought to Jamestown, where they become indentured servants.

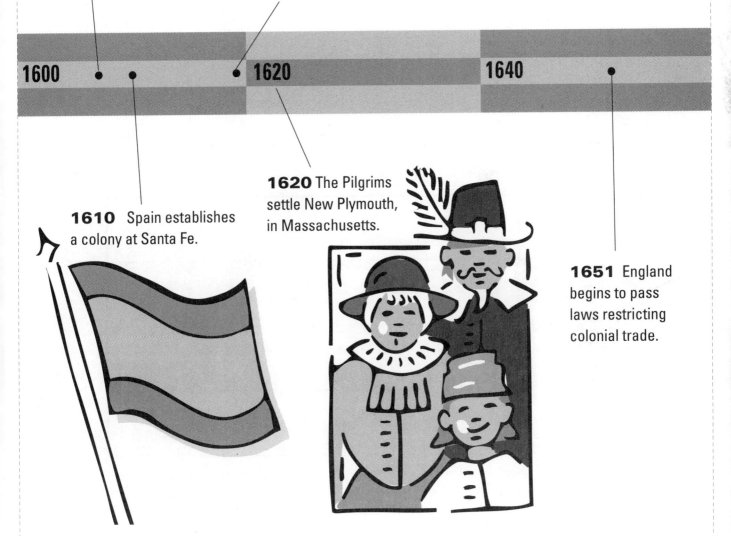

1600

1620

1640

1610 Spain establishes a colony at Santa Fe.

1620 The Pilgrims settle New Plymouth, in Massachusetts.

1651 England begins to pass laws restricting colonial trade.

1718 French settlers found New Orleans.

1680 Pueblo Indians revolt, forcing the Spanish to leave New Mexico.

1660	1680	1700

1700 Population in the English colonies is 275,000.

THOUSANDS OF PEOPLE

| 300 |
| 200 |
| 100 |
| 0 |

1610	1650	1700
210	51,700	275,000

1775 Battles at Lexington and Concord begin the Revolutionary War.

1732 Georgia, the last of the 13 English colonies, is settled.

| 1720 | 1740 | 1760 |

1776 The Declaration of Independence is adopted.

1754 Seven Years' War, or French and Indian War, begins.

American History

1787 The new nation writes a Constitution.

1783 The Treaty of Paris ends the Revolution.

1803 With the Louisiana Purchase, the nation doubles in size.

1825 Erie Canal links east and west.

1780 • • • • 1800 • • 1820 • •

1790 Almost 4 million people live in the new United States, according to the first national census.

1791 Ten amendments—the Bill of Rights—are added to the Constitution.

1812 The United States fights another war with Great Britain.

1830 First wagon train crosses the Rocky Mountains.

1861 The Civil War begins.

1869 A transcontinental railroad links east and west.

1848 At the Seneca Falls convention women declare their rights.

1863 Union soldiers win the Battle of Gettysburg.

1840	**1860**	**1880**

1849 The Gold Rush brings thousands to California.

1865 Confederates surrender at Appomattox, ending the Civil War.

1886 The Statue of Liberty is dedicated.

1876 Alexander Graham Bell invents the telephone.

American History

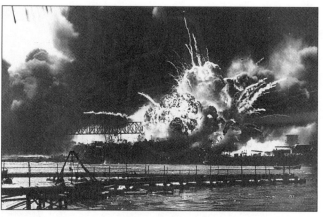

1941 Japan attacks Pearl Harbor and the United States enters World War II.

1958 Explorer I is the nation's first Earth satellite.

1917 The United States enters World War I. The war began in Europe in 1914 and will end in 1918.

1929 The stock market crashes, beginning the Great Depression.

1950 The Korean War begins. It will end in 1953.

1900	1920	1940

1927 Charles Lindbergh flies the first nonstop solo trans-Atlantic flight.

1945 Germany and Japan surrender, ending World War II.
• Delegates from 50 nations form the United Nations.

1954 The Supreme Court outlaws segregated schools.

1959 Alaska and Hawaii become the 49th and 50th states.

1963 Civil rights protestors march in Washington, D.C.

1965 American involvement in Vietnam increases.

1989 The Berlin Wall comes down, signaling the end of the Cold War.

| 1960 | 1980 | 2000 |

1973 Peace treaty ends U.S. involvement in Vietnam; fighting ends two years later.

1976 The nation celebrates its 200th birthday.

1992 The nation marks the 500th anniversary of Columbus's arrival in the Americas.

Exploration

1453 The Ottoman Turks block the overland trade route between Europe and the Far East, leading Europeans to seek new routes.

1492 Christopher Columbus sails from Spain to the Americas, searching for a trade route to the East.

1497 Portuguese explorer Vasco da Gama sails for India with 4 ships and about 150 sailors.
• John Cabot sails from England to Newfoundland, which he thinks is part of Asia.

1487 Bartolmeu Dias sails from Portugal to find a sea route to India.

| 1450 | 1480 | 1485 | 1490 | 1495 |

1488 Dias reaches the Indian Ocean, the first Portuguese sailor to sail around Africa. He returns home before reaching India.

1493 Columbus makes his second voyage to the Americas, where he builds settlements on Hispaniola.

1498 Columbus makes his third trip to the Americas. He returns home in chains, accused of treating people too harshly.
• Da Gama is the first European to reach India by sea.

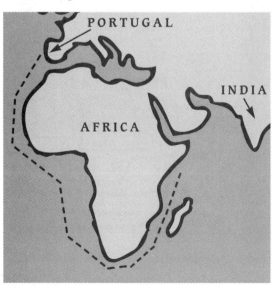

PORTUGAL

INDIA

AFRICA

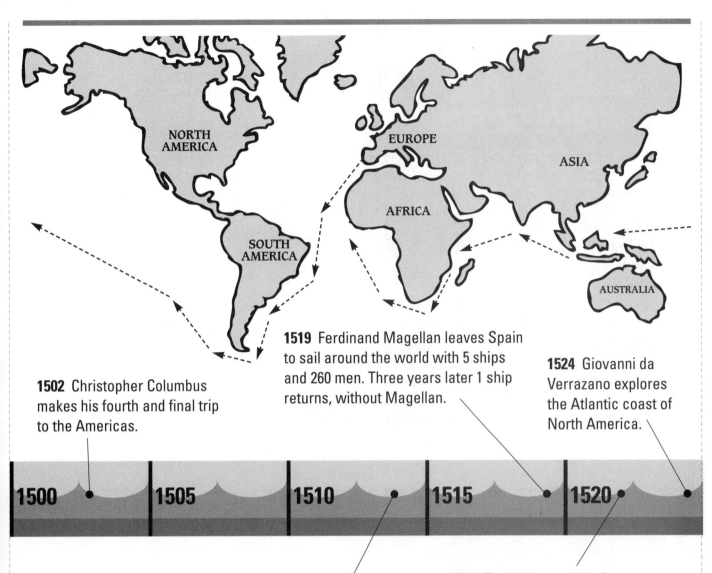

1502 Christopher Columbus makes his fourth and final trip to the Americas.

1519 Ferdinand Magellan leaves Spain to sail around the world with 5 ships and 260 men. Three years later 1 ship returns, without Magellan.

1524 Giovanni da Verrazano explores the Atlantic coast of North America.

1500	1505	1510	1515	1520

1513 Juan Ponce de León names and claims Florida for Spain.

1521 Spanish conquistador Hernan Cortés conquers the Aztec empire in Mexico.

Exploration

1533 In Peru the Inca empire surrenders to conquistador Francisco Pizarro.

1535 Jacques Cartier, a French explorer, searches for a Northwest Passage to Asia and finds the Saint Lawrence River.

1541 Spaniard Fernando de Soto is the first European to cross the Mississippi River.
● Searching for cities of gold, Francisco Vasquez de Coronado reaches what is now Kansas.

1525	1530	1535	1540	1545

1528 A Spanish expedition led by Pánfilo de Narváez explores Florida and the Gulf of Mexico. Storms wreck the fleet.

1536 Alvar Núñez Cabeza de Vaca, a survivor of the Narváez expedition, reaches Mexico after 8 years. He walked more than 1,200 miles.

1542 Juan Cabrillo is the first European to land in what is now California.

1576 Martin Frobisher, an English adventurer, believes that he has found a Northwest Passage to Asia. Instead, he found a bay in Canada.

1577 Sir Francis Drake is the second European to sail around the world. He returns to England 3 years later.

| 1550 | 1575 | 1595 | 1600 | 1605 |

1608 Samuel de Champlain founds Quebec, the first permanent settlement in New France.

1596 Dutch explorers, led by Willem Barents, unsuccessfully seek a Northeast Passage from Asia to Europe. They spend the winter trapped in Arctic ice.

Exploration

1610 Looking for a Northwest Passage to Asia, Henry Hudson sails into what is now Hudson Bay.

1673 French explorers Louis Joliet and Father Jacques Marquette (*right*) travel down the Mississippi River.

1610 | **1670** | **1675** | **1680**

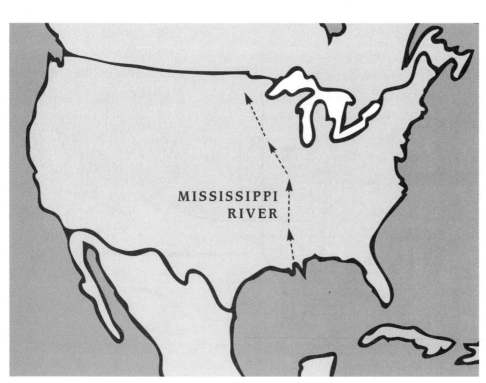

MISSISSIPPI RIVER

1682 Robert Cavelier Sieur de la Salle explores the full length of the Mississippi River and claims the entire region for France.

Growth of the Nation

1607 English settlers begin Jamestown in Virginia, the first permanent English colony in North America.

| 1600 ★ ★ ★ ★ | 1610 ★ ★ ★ ★ |

1610 Spanish build *La Villa Real de la Santa Fe de San Francisco* (Santa Fe) where a Pueblo village once stood.

1619 20 Africans are brought to Jamestown, where they become indentured servants.

Growth of the Nation

1620 The *Mayflower* brings 50 men, 20 women, and 32 children to build a new English colony at New Plymouth.

1624 30 Dutch families settle New Netherland.

History Mystery

• Just Arrived! What has 4 legs and gives you something good to drink?

1638 Swedish settlers begin colony of New Sweden.
• First printing press arrives from England.

History Mystery

• For Rent: The first log cabins in America. Who built them and where?

1632 English Catholics begin Maryland colony.

1620 ★ ★ ★ ★ **1630** ★ ★ ★ ★

1621 At New Plymouth the Pilgrims and the Wampanoag celebrate a feast of thanksgiving for those who survived the winter.

1636 Roger Williams and Puritans begin the Rhode Island colony, the first to give complete religious freedom to all.

1640 First book— the *Bay Psalm Book*— is published in the colonies.

1645 American slave ships leave Boston for West Africa.

1654 24 Jewish immigrants arrive in the colonies.

1640 ★ ★ ★ ★ **1650** ★ ★ ★ ★

1643 First American word book is published —a dictionary of Native American languages.

1653 North Carolina colony is settled by Virginia colonists.
• The Iroquois League signs a peace treaty with the French.

1646 To prevent fires, Boston out- laws smoking within 5 miles of town.

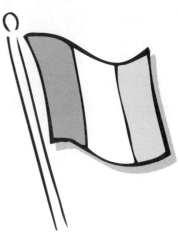

Growth of the Nation

1661 The first Bible is published in the colonies, a translation into the Algonquian language.

1674 French missionary Jacques Marquette establishes a mission on one of the Great Lakes claimed by the French 3 years earlier. (Now it's Chicago.)

1660 ★ ★ ★ ★ **1670** ★ ★ ★ ★ ★

1664 English nobles turn New Netherland into New York and begin the New Jersey colony.
• The colonies begin passing laws that limit the possibility of freedom for enslaved Africans.

1670 English colonists settle the South Carolina colony.

History Mystery

1673 Got a Pen? Why should you write more letters now?

1680 New Hampshire separates from Massachusetts to become a colony.

1690 A big year for paper: the first newspaper and the first paper money are issued in Massachusetts.

1692 20 people in Salem, Massachusetts, are executed as witches.

1680 ★ ★ ★ ★ **1690** ★ ★ ★ ★

1681 Quaker William Penn receives a charter for a new colony, which will become Pennsylvania.

History Mystery

1699 Find the Hidden Treasure! What did pirate Captain Kidd bury and where?

Growth of the Nation

1700 First published attack on slavery, *The Selling of Joseph,* appears.

HistoryMystery

1706 Poor Richard! What famous almanac writer, kite flyer, and Declaration signer was born in Boston?

1700 ★ ★ ★ ★ **1710** ★ ★ ★ ★

1701 Delaware becomes a separate colony.

1718 New Orleans is founded by French settlers from France and Canada.

1732 James Oglethorpe (*right*) founds Georgia, the 13th English colony, as a refuge for debtors.

History Mystery

• Watch that cherry tree! Whose "Father" was born in Virginia on February 22?

1720 Population of English colonies is almost 475,000—up from 275,000 in 1700.

1725 Population of enslaved Africans in English colonies reaches 75,000.

1720 ★ ★ ★ ★ **1730** ★ ★ ★ ★

1723 Colonies fear rising crime—Boston's -12-man police force is told "to walke Silently and Slowly, now and then to Stand Still and Listen in order to make discovery."

1731 Benjamin Franklin opens first circulating library in the Americas.

1735 John Peter Zenger is declared innocent in an important test of freedom of the press.

History Mystery

1752 Go Fly a Kite! What did Benjamin Franklin find out when he did?

1749 Two New Englanders begin first English settlement west of the Allegheny Mountains.

1740 ★ ★ ★ ★ ★ **1750** ★ ★ ★ ★ ★

1754 The French and Indian War begins when French and British soldiers battle at Fort Duquesne (now Pittsburgh).
• The Albany Congress is the first attempt to unite the 13 colonies.

1773 In a midnight "tea party," Bostonians defy British tea taxes by dumping 342 chests of tea into Boston Harbor.

1763 The Treaty of Paris ends the French and Indian War, giving Great Britain control of Canada and all land east of the Mississippi.

1769 In California, Spanish priest Father Junipero Serra establishes the first mission, *San Diego de Alcala.*

History Mystery

1777 Thirteen stars and thirteen stripes— What did Congress approve this year?

1760 ★ ★ ★ ★ 1770 ★ ★ ★ ★

1765 British Parliament passes the Stamp Act, which taxes angry colonists.

1770 In Boston, British troops and colonists clash in the "Boston Massacre."

1776 Declaration of Independence is signed in Philadelphia.

1767 Daniel Boone first explores land west of the Appalachian Mountains.

1775 Hear This! Patrick Henry speaks out against Great Britain.
• Fighting at Lexington and Concord begins the American Revolution.
• In Philadelphia Ben Franklin and others form the first organization to abolish slavery.

Growth of the Nation

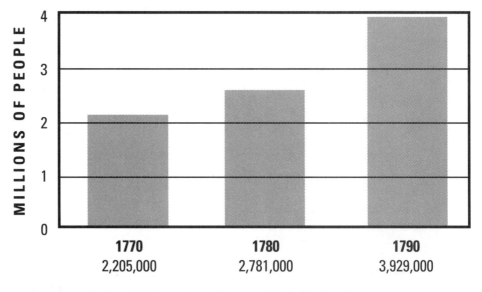

1789 The Constitution, written in 1787, becomes the law of the land.
• George Washington is inaugurated as first President.

1780 **1790**

1790 According to the first U.S. Census the nation's population is almost 4 million people.

1783 The United States and Great Britain sign the Treaty of Paris to end the American Revolution.

MILLIONS OF PEOPLE

1770	1780	1790
2,205,000	2,781,000	3,929,000

POPULATION OF THE UNITED STATES: 1770 to 1790

1801 Thomas Jefferson is first U.S. President inaugurated in the new capital, Washington, DC.

1809 Abraham Lincoln is born in Kentucky.

HistoryMystery

1814 Oh Say Can You Guess? What important song did Francis Scott Key write during the War of 1812?

1800 ★ ★ ★ ★ 1810 ★ ★ ★ ★

1808 Congress stops the African slave trade, making it illegal to import slaves.

1810 King Kamehameha unites the Hawaiian Islands.

1803 Lewis and Clark set out to explore the Louisiana Purchase, the 828,000 square miles of land President Jefferson has added to the United States.

Growth of the Nation

1821 Travelers leaving Independence, Missouri, spend 40-60 days to reach Santa Fe, a journey of 780 miles.
• Emma Willard opens the first college for women in Troy, New York.

1826 Founding Fathers Thomas Jefferson and John Adams die on July 4, 50 years after signing the Declaration of Independence.

1829 The railroad age begins when the Baltimore and Ohio Railroad carries passengers on its first 13 miles of track.

1820 ★ ★ ★ ★ 1830 ★ ★ ★ ★

1824 Sequoyah, a Cherokee Indian, completes the first written alphabet for an American Indian language.

1828 20 years in the making, Noah Webster's *American Dictionary of the English Language* is published.

1834 Cyrus McCormick patents the reaper that will revolutionize agriculture.

1838 The U.S. government forces 14,000 Cherokee Indians from their east coast homes, sending them along a "Trail of Tears" to Oklahoma.

1825 The Erie Canal officially opens, a 363-mile link that allows boats to travel from the Great Lakes to the Hudson River and on to the Atlantic Ocean.

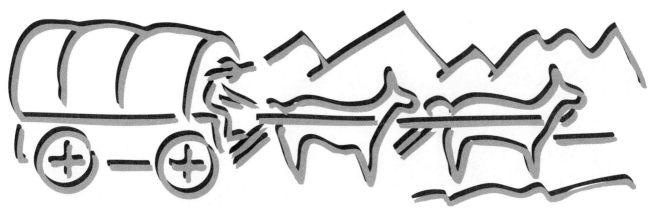

1841 The first wagon train to California leaves Kansas in May, reaching Sonora the following November.

1848 Meeting in Seneca Falls, NY, 300 women declare that women deserve the same rights as men.

1853 Sailing into Tokyo Bay, Commodore Matthew Perry "opens the door" to trade between Japan and the world for the first time since 1683.

1840

1850

HistoryMystery

1844 Dot dash dot— Samuel F. B. Morse sent a speedy message. How did he do it and what did he say?

1849 80,000 people rush to California to find gold—$10 million worth this year alone.

HistoryMystery

1859 Black Gold! 20 barrels a day flow in Titusville, PA. What is it?

1846 In the first recorded baseball game, the New York Nine beat the Knickerbockers 23 to 1.

Growth of the Nation

1861 The Civil War begins on April 12 when Confederate forces fire on Fort Sumter in Charleston, SC.

1865 The bloody Civil War ends, with more than 2 million Americans killed or wounded.
• Abraham Lincoln is assassinated in Washington, DC.
• The Thirteenth Amendment to the Constitution prohibits slavery.

1872 Yellowstone National Park is established, the first national park.

1876 Alexander Graham Bell patents the first telephone.

History Mystery

• Happy Birthday to US! Whose birthday is celebrated by almost 10 million visitors in Philadelphia?

1860 **1870**

1862 The Homestead Act grants 160 acres of free land to anyone over 21. More than 2 million people will claim land and build new lives in the West.

1866 A new coin appears—the first nickels are made.

1877 Reconstruction ends as the last federal soldiers withdraw from the South.

1863 With the Emancipation Proclamation President Lincoln promises freedom to enslaved African Americans in the Confederate states.

1879 Thomas Edison invents the first practical electric lights.

1891 A Massachusetts physical education teacher invents the game of basketball.

1886 The 225-ton, 152-foot-tall Statue of Liberty is dedicated in New York harbor.

1892 Charles and Frank Duryea, brothers and bicycle makers, build the first successful gasoline-powered automobile.

1880 ★ ★ ★ ★ **1890** ★ ★ ★ ★

1884 The first skyscrapers are built, made possible by the development of steel structures and elevators.

1898 The United States takes over Puerto Rico, the Philippine Islands, and Guam in the Spanish American War.

1896 At the first modern Olympic Games, U.S. teams win 9 out of 12 events.

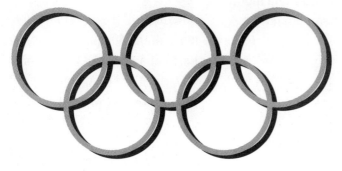

Growth of the Nation

1900 When the Automobile Club of America holds its first auto show, only 8,000 cars are registered in the nation. (At the time there are 18 million horses and mules and 10 million bicycles).

1913 Henry Ford revolutionizes manufacturing with the first assembly-line system for making his Model T cars.

1918 World War I ends at 11:00 on the eleventh day of the eleventh month.
• Almost 500,000 Americans die in a nationwide flu epidemic.

1900   **1910**

1903 Orville Wright makes the first airplane flight at Kitty Hawk, NC, after years of work with his brother Wilbur.
• Baseball's first World Series takes place between the Pittsburgh Pirates and the Boston Red Sox.

History Mystery

1909 Brrr—it's cold here! What spot did Robert E. Peary and Matthew Henson reach after one month on the ice?

1917 The United States enters World War I.

1914 The Panama Canal opens officially, after workers have dug up more than 240 million cubic yards of earth at a cost of $366 million.
• World War I begins, but the United States remains neutral.

1920 The first airmail service carries mail from New York to San Francisco in four days.

History Mystery

1927 Lucky Lindy! Who was he and what did he do in 33 1/2 hours?

1933 One out of four Americans is out of work as newly elected President Franklin Roosevelt begins his New Deal programs.

1939 World War II begins in Europe, but the United States remains neutral.

1920 ★ ★ ★ ★ **1930** ★ ★ ★ ★

1929 The first Academy Awards are presented.
• The stock market crashes and the Great Depression begins.

1937 Pioneering pilot Amelia Earhart is reported lost over the Pacific.

1922 The Nineteenth Amendment to the Constitution grants women the right to vote.

Growth of the Nation

1941 The United States enters the war after Japan attacks Pearl Harbor.

1945 World War II ends with unconditional surrender by Germany and Japan.
• Delegates from 50 nations meet in San Francisco to form the United Nations.

1950 The Korean War begins and the U.S. sends troops to support South Korea after North Korean invasion.

1954 Outlawing the "separate but equal" policy, the Supreme Court declares racial segregation in public schools unconstitutional.

1940

1950

1944 Allied forces land at Normandy in France, a turning point in the war.

1946 Scientists have developed a new, 30-ton machine—ENIAC, the first electronic digital computer.

1953 Korean War ends.

1959 Alaska and Hawaii are admitted as 49th and 50th states.

1942 The first American jet airplane is tested.

1958 America's Space Age begins as the U.S. launches first Earth satellite, Explorer I.

1968 Martin Luther King, Jr., and Robert F. Kennedy are assassinated.

1975 The Vietnam War, the nation's longest war, ends with South Vietnam's surrender to the Communist Vietcong forces.

History Mystery

1962 Hello down there! Who is the first American to orbit Earth?

1964 Congress passes far-reaching Civil Rights Act.
• The Surgeon General warns Americans of the dangers of cigarette smoking.

1971 The 26th Amendment lowers voting age from 21 to 18.

History Mystery

1976 Two centuries young! What anniversary is celebrated this year?

1960

1970

1963 U.S. President John F. Kennedy is assassinated.
• More than 200,000 peaceful protestors hear Martin Luther King, Jr., and other civil rights leaders in a Freedom March in Washington, DC.

1965 Thousands of Americans march from Selma to Montgomery, Alabama, as racial tensions and civil rights struggles continue.

1969 Hundreds of thousands of anti-war protestors gather in Washington, DC, and San Francisco.
• Neil Armstrong is the first person to set foot on the moon, taking "one giant leap for mankind."

1974 Richard Nixon is the first American President to resign.

1979 Revolutionaries in Iran take U.S. citizens hostage—they will not be free until 1981.

Growth of the Nation

1981 The introduction of personal computers begins a revolution in offices, homes, and schools.

1984 Doctors identify the virus that causes AIDS.

1986 The Challenger shuttle explodes, killing 7 astronauts.

1990 For the first time a majority of Americans live in metropolitan areas.
• Congress passes act to prevent discrimination against the disabled.

1980 ★ ★ ★ ★ **1990** ★ ★ ★ ★

1989 U.S. and Soviet leaders agree that the Cold War is over.

1991 U.S. troops support Kuwait against Iraq as the Persian Gulf War begins and ends quickly.

1992 On the 500th anniversary of Columbus's landing, Americans rethink the roles of Native Americans and explorers.

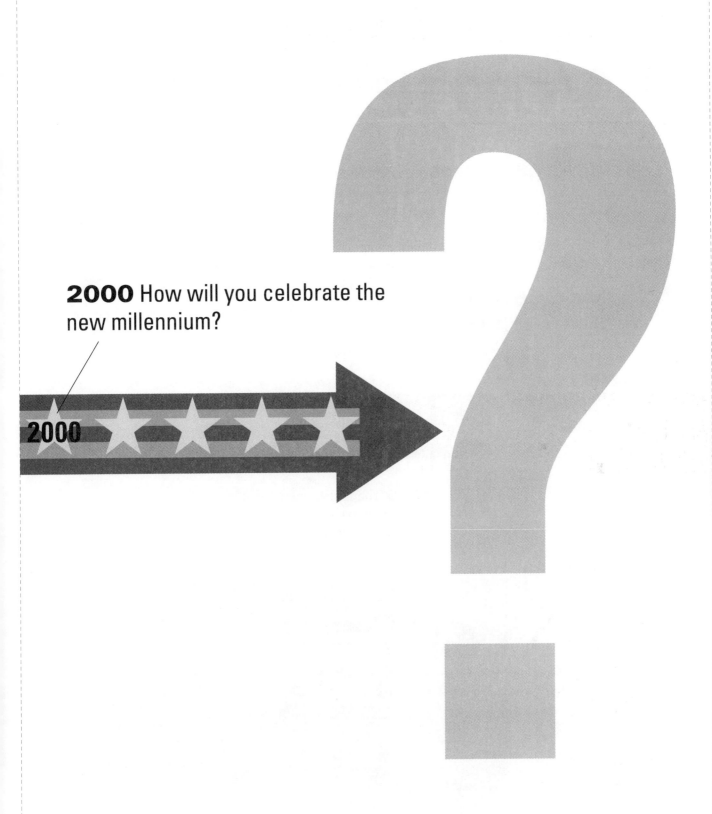

2000 How will you celebrate the new millennium?

2000

American Women

1608 In colonial Virginia, Pocahantas—daughter of Powhatan chief Wahunsonacook—uses her influence to save the life of Captain John Smith.

1620 20 women are among the 102 passengers on the *Mayflower*.

1600   **1620**

1619 The first women arrive in the Jamestown colony: 90 English women and 3 African women.

1638 Banished from Massachusetts, religious leader Anne Hutchinson sets up a new community in Rhode Island.

1648 Margaret Brent, one of Maryland's largest landowners, demands the right to vote but the Assembly refuses.

1692 In Salem, Massachusetts, 20 women are accused of witchcraft and killed.

| 1640 | • | 1660 | 1680 | • | • |

1683 Giulielma Maria Penn begins work with her husband William to create the Pennsylvania colony.

1660 Mary Dyer is hanged in Boston for refusing to give up her Quaker faith.

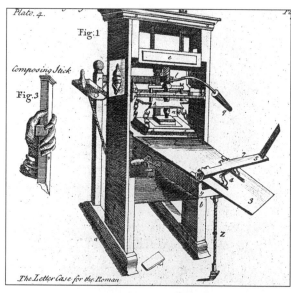

1715 New Jersey colonist Sybilla Masters receives a patent for a machine to process corn.

1735 Read all about it! Printer Ann Franklin publishes newspapers, colonial documents, and the almanacs of her brother-in-law Ben.

1700   1720   1740

1733 Creek Indian interpreter Mary Musgrove aids Georgia founder James Oglethorpe.

1741 In South Carolina Eliza Lucas introduces the cultivation of indigo, which will become a major export crop.

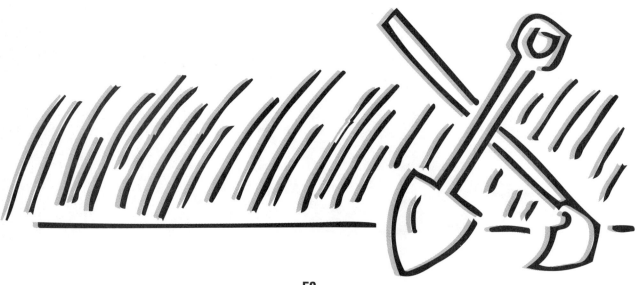

1772 Mercy Otis Warren publishes a play making fun of the British Governor.

1776 "Remember the ladies"! Abigail Adams urges husband John to create fair laws for the new nation.

1782 Teacher Deborah Sampson, disguised in men's clothes, fights as a Revolutionary soldier for 18 months.

1814 First Lady Dolley Madison rescues White House valuables in the War of 1812.
• Women begin work in textile mills, soon producing 30 miles of cloth per day.

1760 • • • •   **1780** •   •   **1800** •   •

1773 The poems of Phillis Wheatley are published in London, a year after she was freed from slavery.

1775 Chief Nancy Ward urges the Cherokee not to take sides in British-colonial conflict.

1778 Molly Pitcher (Mary Hays McCaulay) brings water to thirsty Continental soldiers, takes over a cannon, and earns the rank of sergeant.

1792 Katherine Greene sponsors Eli Whitney's invention of the cotton gin.

1805 Sacajawea, a Shoshone Indian, interprets for explorers Lewis and Clark.

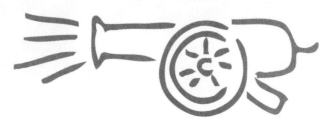

American Women

1828 On time or else! First strike by women workers protests severe wage cuts for 5-minute lateness.

1832 Female Anti-Slavery Society founded by women of color in Salem, Massachusetts.

1843 Dorothea Dix begins 40-year campaign to improve treatment of mental patients.

1848 300 delegates at Seneca Falls Woman's Rights Convention adopt a Declaration of Sentiments.

1852 Harriet Beecher Stowe's *Uncle Tom's Cabin* is published.

1863 Thanksgiving becomes a national holiday due to efforts of magazine editor Sarah Josepha Hale.

1820 • • • • • 1840 • • • • 1860 • •

1829 The Grimke sisters begin lifelong campaigns for women's rights and against slavery.

1836 Narcissa Whitman and Eliza Spalding are first white women to cross the American continent.

1839 Mississippi passes first U.S. law allowing married women to own property.

1849 Elizabeth Blackwell is the first woman to receive a degree as doctor of medicine.
• Harriet Tubman begins a rescue operation that will lead about 300 people from slavery to freedom.

1869 Lucy Stone, Susan B. Anthony (*below*), and Elizabeth Cady Stanton found national associations for women's suffrage.
• Wyoming territory is first to give women the right to vote.

1881
Former teacher Clara Barton founds American Red Cross.

1904 Helen Keller, blind and deaf, graduates from college and begins her career.
• Black educator Mary McLeod Bethune opens a training school in Florida.

1889
Newspaper-woman Nellie Bly travels around the world in a record 72 days, 6 hours, 11 minutes, 14 seconds.

1912
The Girl Guides (later the Girl Scouts) is founded.

1924 In Texas "Ma" Ferguson becomes nation's first woman elected governor.

1932 Pilot Amelia Earhart is the first woman to fly the Atlantic solo.

1920
American women win the right to vote when the 19th amendment to the Constitution is passed.

1931 Jane Addams, founder of Hull House, receives Nobel Peace Prize.

1880 • • •

1900 • •   • • •

1920 • •   • •   •

1902
Journalist Ida Tarbell's articles expose wrongs in American business.

1913 5,000 suffragettes march in Washington to demand the vote.

1926 Gertrude Ederle swims the English Channel in 14 1/2 hours.

1911 More than 140 young women die in Triangle Shirtwaist Factory fire.

1916
Montana elects nation's first Congress-woman, Jeanette Rankin.

1939 Marian Anderson sings at the Lincoln Memorial before a crowd of 75,000.

1885 Annie Oakley stuns world with her shooting skills in Buffalo Bill's Wild West Show.

American Women

1954 The right of Linda Carol Brown to attend her neighborhood school is at the heart of the Supreme Court case *Brown v. Board of Education* which declared school segregation illegal.

1978 At the largest women's meeting in the world, almost 100,000 demonstrators in Washington support ratification of an Equal Rights Amendment.
• For the first time, more women than men enter colleges in the U.S.

1981 Sandra Day O'Connor becomes the first woman justice on the Supreme Court.

1984 Geraldine Ferraro is the first woman to run for Vice President on a major party ticket.

1942 Women join the war effort as WAACs, WAVES, and WASPs.

1962 Labor organizer Dolores Huerta plays an important role in founding the United Farm Workers.

1966 The National Organization for Women is founded.

1940 • • •   **1960** • • • •   **1980** • • • •

1964 The Civil Rights Act forbids discrimination against women in the workplace.

1983 Sally Ride, America's first woman astronaut, spends 6 days in a space shuttle.

1993 Take Our Daughters to Work Day urges Americans to introduce young girls to the workplace.

1953 Pilot Jacqueline Cochran is the first woman to break the sound barrier.

AFRICAN AMERICAN HISTORY

1502 Spanish settlers bring enslaved Africans to the Americas.

1526 Africans accompany Spanish explorers to an area now part of South Carolina.

1600 More than 900,000 enslaved Africans live in Latin America.

1500

1600

1513 30 Africans are part of Vasco Nunez Balboa's expedition to find the Pacific Ocean.

1619 20 African indentured servants are brought to Jamestown, Virginia, on a Dutch ship.

1538 The explorer Estavanico, once enslaved, leads an expedition from Mexico into the American Southwest, seeking the Seven Cities of Gold.

AFRICAN AMERICAN HISTORY

1624 William Tucker is the first African child born in the English colonies.

1641 Massachusetts becomes the first English colony to legalize slavery.

1651 Anthony Johnson, a free black, tries to form an independent African community in Virginia.

1664 Colonial laws begin to limit possibilities of freedom for enslaved Africans.

1688 A Mennonite resolution against slavery is the first formal protest in the Western Hemisphere.

1630 In Massachusetts a law is passed to protect slaves from "abusive owners."

1645 The slave trade is a profitable business in New England, where ships leave Boston for the West African coast.

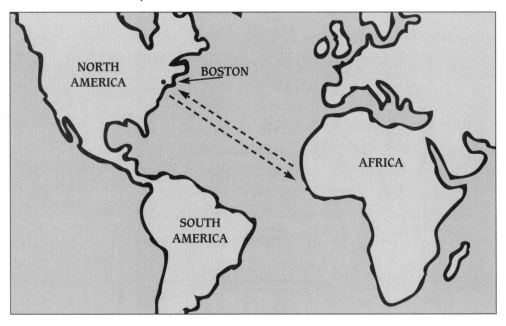

1746 Enslaved poet Lucy Terry writes "Bars Fight," about the Deerfield Massacre.

1700 Judge Samuel Sewall publishes *The Selling of Joseph*, denouncing slavery.

1700

1725 75,000 enslaved Africans live in the English colonies.

1754 Benjamin Banneker, a 22-year-old free black, makes the first clock built in the colonies.

1769 Thomas Jefferson is unsuccessful in efforts to persuade Virginia's legislature to free enslaved African Americans.

1770 Among the first casualties in the American Revolution, African American sailor Crispus Attucks dies in the Boston Massacre.

1774 The Continental Congress proposes eliminating the slave trade.

1776 The Declaration of Independence is signed, without Thomas Jefferson's proposed denouncement of slavery.

1787 The 13 states adopt the U.S. Constitution, which allows the slave trade to continue until 1808.

1790 The first U.S. Census counts 757,000 African Americans who make up 19% of the population. About 68,000 are free.

1793 Congress passes the Fugitive Slave Act, making it a crime to hide or protect an escaped slave.

1773 *Poems on Various Subjects, Religious and Moral*, a collection of poems by Phillis Wheatley, is published in London.

1775 The Continental Congress forbids African Americans from serving in the armed forces.
• In Philadelphia the first abolitionist society is formed.
• General George Washington later allows free blacks to serve in the Revolutionary army, the first of 10,000 who will fight against the British.

1791 Benjamin Banneker is part of the commission that plans Washington, DC, the nation's new capital.

1800 Free blacks in Philadelphia petition Congress to end slavery gradually, but their petition is rejected 85-1.

1816 The American Colonization Society is organized to send free blacks to Africa, although many free blacks are opposed. In six years the society will help found the African nation of Liberia.

1827 The nation's first African American newspaper, *Freedom's Journal*, begins publication.

1800

1808 Congress forbids slave trade in the U.S. At the time there are about 1 million enslaved African Americans in the nation.

1822 Southern states pass stricter laws limiting movement of African Americans after a revolt led by enslaved Denmark Vesey.

1831 Nat Turner leads a major rebellion against slavery in Virginia.

1838 The Supreme Court awards freedom to Joseph Cinque and other Africans who were aboard the *Amistad.*

1849 Harriet Tubman escapes from slavery. She will transport more than 300 slaves to freedom on the Underground Railroad.

1861 The Civil War begins. Almost 180,000 African Americans will serve in the Union Army.

1865 When the Civil War is over, the 13th Amendment to the Constitution ends slavery.

1847 Frederick Douglass publishes first issues of *The North Star,* his newspaper focused on abolition.
• Dred Scott claims his freedom from slavery in the St. Louis courts. Ten years later the Supreme Court will deny his rights to citizenship.

1852 Sojourner Truth speaks before a national convention on women's rights.
• Publication of *Uncle Tom's Cabin* supports the anti-slavery movement. The book sells 300,000 copies in the first year.

1863 The Emancipation Proclamation promises freedom for slaves in Confederate states.

1870 Representative Joseph Rainey of South Carolina and Senator Hiram Revels of Mississippi are the first African Americans to serve in Congress.

1896 In *Plessy v. Ferguson* the Supreme Court upholds segregation, saying "separate but equal" facilities are constitutional.

1881 The beginning of "Jim Crow" laws brings greater segregation in the South.
• Booker T. Washington (*left*) opens Tuskegee Institute in Alabama.

1915 Boll weevils destroy cotton crops, causing great migration of blacks from the South to the North.

1926 A. Philip Randolph founds Brotherhood of Sleeping Car Porters.
• Negro History Week is introduced.

1900 Scholar W. E. B. DuBois attends first Pan-African Congress.

1925 The literary anthology *The New Negro* highlights the Harlem Renaissance.

1900

1909 Matthew Henson, with Admiral Robert Peary's expedition, places U.S. flag at North Pole.
• W. E. B. DuBois publishes first issue of *Crisis*, the magazine of the newly formed NAACP.

1936 Athlete Jesse Owens wins 4 medals at the Olympic Games in Berlin.

1960 "Sit-in" protests across the South begin at segregated lunch counters in North Carolina.

1939 At the Lincoln Memorial Marian Anderson sings before a crowd of 75,000 on Easter Sunday.

1941 Dr. Charles R. Drew sets up the nation's first blood bank.

1954 In *Brown v. the Board of Education* the Supreme Court says segregated public schools are unconstitutional.

1940 Benjamin O. Davis becomes the first black general in the nation's armed forces.

1950 Diplomat Ralph Bunche wins the Nobel Peace Prize.

1957 A major civil rights confrontation takes place in Little Rock, Arkansas, as 9 black students integrate Central High School.

1955 Led by Martin Luther King, Jr., and others in Montgomery, Alabama, black citizens boycott city buses.

1963 More than 250,000 marching for civil rights in Washington, DC, hear Martin Luther King, Jr.'s "I Have a Dream" speech.

1964 Landmark civil rights law to prevent segregation in public housing and employment is signed by President Lyndon Johnson.
• Martin Luther King, Jr., wins Nobel Peace Prize.

1968 Martin Luther King, Jr., is assassinated.

1983 The third Monday in January becomes a federal holiday to honor Martin Luther King, Jr.

1965 Voting Rights Act is passed to prevent voter discrimination.
• Black leader Malcolm X is assassinated.

1967 Racial conflicts create a "long hot summer" with rioting in major cities.
• Thurgood Marshall (*right*) becomes the first black justice on the Supreme Court.

1970 Black legislators form the Congressional Black Caucus.

1992 Mae Jemison is the first African American woman in space.

Science & Technology

1612 Virginia colonists begin making bricks.

1621 The first blast furnace is built in Virginia.

1631 The first ship built in America is christened *Blessing of the Bay.*

1610	1620	1630

1613 The Jamestown colony is saved when colonists learn to grow tobacco which they can sell to England.

1639 Colonists set up first printing press, at Harvard College.

1624 The first cattle arrive in the English colonies.

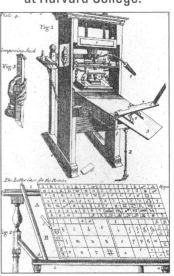

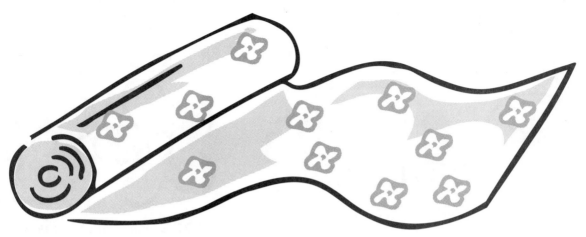

1643 The first mill to make woolen cloth is built in Massachusetts.

1644 America's first successful iron works is built near Boston.

| 1640 | | 1650 | | 1660 |

1659 Joseph Jenks builds the first "fire engine," a portable water pump.

Science & Technology

1690 Two Americans build the first American paper mill near Philadelphia.

1728 John Bartram creates the first botanical gardens in America.
• A Connecticut blacksmith produces the first American steel.

1724 South Carolinians begin irrigating rice fields.

| 1690 | 1720 • • • | 1730 • |

1721 Boston doctor is the first American to vaccinate patients against smallpox.

1738 The first successful glass factory starts in New Jersey.

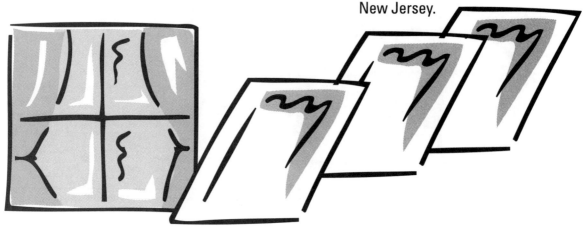

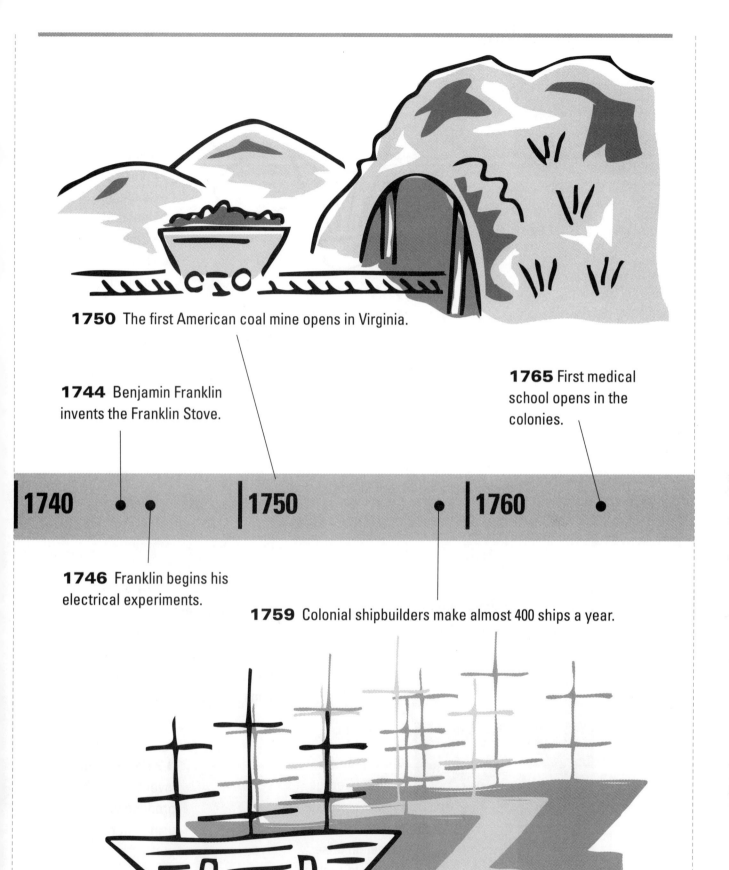

1750 The first American coal mine opens in Virginia.

1765 First medical school opens in the colonies.

1744 Benjamin Franklin invents the Franklin Stove.

| 1740 | 1750 | 1760 |

1746 Franklin begins his electrical experiments.

1759 Colonial shipbuilders make almost 400 ships a year.

Science & Technology

1770 Benjamin Banneker builds wooden clock that will keep time for more than 50 years.

1775 American invents one-person submarine called the "American Turtle."

1784 A 13-year-old boy is first person to make balloon flight in America.
• First automatic production line is set up in a flour mill.

1789 First American road map is published.

1790 Samuel Slater builds steam-powered machines to process cotton and starts the Industrial Revolution in the United States.
• Congress rejects Thomas Jefferson's suggestion that the nation adopt the metric system.
• The first American patent is awarded, for a manufacturing process.

1770   1780   1790

1773 Inventor suggests a steam-powered "horse-less carriage."

1783 The first map of the United States is made.

1787 First American steamboat is launched.
• First American cotton mill opens.

1793 Eli Whitney invents the cotton gin.

1785 George Washington's dentist makes the first porcelain false teeth—to replace the wooden ones.

1798 Eli Whitney invents a machine to produce weapons, using interchangeable parts, the beginning of mass production.

1814 Francis Lowell opens nation's first totally mechanized factory, to make cloth from raw cotton.

1827 Audubon publishes *Birds of America* with 435 drawings.

1817 Construction of Erie Canal begins, to connect the Great Lakes to the Atlantic (via the Hudson River). The canal will be completed 8 years later.

1829 Jacob Bigelow invents the word "technology."

1825 A canner patents the first tin cans.

1800   **1810**   **1820**

1807 Robert Fulton launches his steamboat *Clermont*, traveling 150 miles in 32 hours.

1821 A Rhode Island inventor develops first hot-air heating system for homes.
• A 450-foot tunnel—the nation's first—opens in Pennsylvania.

1826 An internal combustion engine is patented.

1828 American physicist invents the electromagnet.

Science & Technology

1830 Peter Cooper builds nation's first successful steam locomotive, but it loses a race to a horse!

1832 Samuel F. B. Morse designs the telegraph machine.

1838 Morse introduces a special code for sending messages on the telegraph.

1851 Isaac Singer patents a successful sewing machine.

1858 The first successful transatlantic telegraph cable is laid.

1830 • • • • | **1840** | **1850** • •

1831 Joseph Henry makes the first electric motor.

1839 Inventor Charles Goodyear discovers a process for making rubber usable.

1852 Elisha Otis invents a passenger elevator.

1834 Cyrus McCormick patents his reaper.

1876 Alexander Graham Bell patents the telephone.

1879 Edison invents the first practical electric light.

1881 A Connecticut inventor creates the first color photographs.

1866 A Connecticut manufacturer invents a steam automobile.

1860	1870	1880

1869 East-west tracks meet in Utah to complete the world's first transcontinental railroad.

1878 Inventor Thomas Alva Edison patents the phonograph, recording "Mary had a little lamb."

1884 The first practical fountain pen is made.

Science & Technology

1903 Orville and Wilbur Wright are the first to fly successfully in a motorized airplane.

1908 47-story skyscraper is built in New York.
• Electric irons and toasters are patented.

1911 The air conditioner is invented.

1926 Robert Goddard launches the first liquid-fuel rocket.
• First full-length talking picture is released.

1900 • • •   **1910** • • •   **1920**   • • •

1905 The first direct blood transfusion takes place.

1910 Electric washing machines are invented.

1915 First transcontinental telephone call.

1927 The first practical television is demonstrated.

1913 The X-ray process is developed.

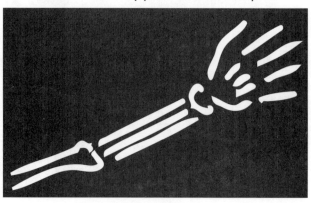

1929 Clarence Birdseye introduces commercial frozen foods.

1945 The first atomic bomb is exploded at a test site.

1947 An electronic calculator is developed.
• A rocket-powered airplane makes the first supersonic flight.

1954 Widespread vaccination against polio begins.
• Plastic contact lenses are produced.

1938 The first product made of nylon—a toothbrush—is on the market.

1941 Government OKs TV broadcasting. 1 million sets sold in the first year.

1950 Networks begin color television broadcasts.

1930   **1940**   **1950**

1943 Large-scale production of penicillin begins the successful use of antibiotics.

1951 The first video cameras record pictures and sound on magnetic tape.

1939 The first color television is demonstrated.
• The first practical helicopter is made.

1946 ENIAC—Electronic Numerical Integrator Calculator—is the first electronic digital computer.

1948 The transistor is invented.
• The first long-playing records are made.

1958 The first photocopying machines are marketed.
• Stereo recordings are introduced.
• Nation launches first space satellite.

Science & Technology

1960
A nuclear submarine circles the globe under-water.

1970 Americans observe first Earth Day to show concern for environmental pollution.

1964 Surgeon general's report points to dangers of cigarette smoking.

1984 Scientists identify virus that causes AIDS.

1986 New technology for VCRs and CDs leads to boom-ing sales.

1981 Introduction of personal computers will revolutionize computer use.

1960	1970	1980

1963 Doctor develops a mechanical heart.

1969 The Internet, a worldwide network linking computers, is created.

1982 Patient receives world's first successful artificial heart transplant.

1985 225-million-year old-dinosaur skeleton found in Arizona.

1972 U.S. bans use of DDT.

1967 Computers first create electronic music.
• The 100 millionth telephone is installed in the United States.
• Synthetic DNA is made in a laboratory.

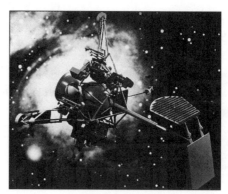

1988 Astronomers detect objects in the universe estimated to be 17 billion years old.

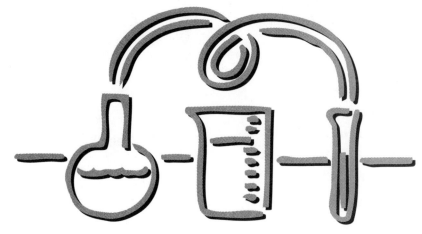

1991 U.S. issues its 5 millionth patent—for a genetically engineered microbe.

1995 The World Wide Web, created in 1990, is the fastest growing service on the Internet.

| 1990 • • • | 2000 |

1992 A 10-year project seeking life on other worlds begins at giant telescopes in Puerto Rico and California.

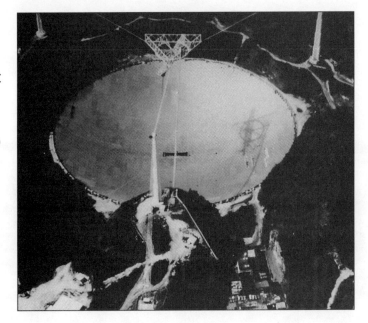

Space

1958 United States enters the space race by setting up NASA—the National Aeronautics and Space Administration.

- Explorer I, the nation's first satellite, makes an unmanned space trip.

1961 Alan Shepard, the first American in space, makes a 15-minute flight on Freedom 7.

- President Kennedy promises to land "an American on the moon in this decade."

1958	1959	1960	1961

1960 The first weather satellite is launched.

1959 NASA chooses the first seven astronauts.

- Explorer VI takes the first TV pictures of Earth.
- Two monkeys travel 300 miles above Earth.

1962 John Glenn is the first American to orbit Earth. He makes 3 orbits—81,000 miles—on Friendship 7.

1969 Neil Armstrong takes "one small step for a man, one giant leap for mankind" when he is the first person ever to walk on the moon.

1966 After landing on the moon, unmanned Surveyor 1 sends back more than 11,000 photograhs.

1962	1963	1964	1965	1966	1967	1968	1969

1965 Edward White, the first American to walk in space, spends 23 minutes outside of Gemini 4.

1967 Three astronauts die in Apollo launch pad fire.

• Unmanned Surveyor 6 lands on the moon, lifts off, and lands again.

1968 Three astronauts circle the moon 10 times, the first manned lunar orbit.

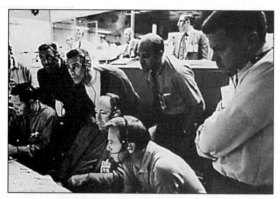

1970 Three astronauts return safely to Earth when mechanical failure forces Apollo 13 to cancel moon landing.

1976 Vikings 1 and 2 land on Mars.

| 1970 | 1971 | 1972 | 1973 | 1974 | 1975 | 1976 | 1977 |

1972 Astronauts on Apollo 17 spend 75 hours on the moon as the last Americans to land on the moon.

1977 The first space shuttle, Enterprise, makes successful test flights.

1971 Mariner 9 orbits Mars.
• Astronauts drive a Lunar Rover 17 miles on the moon.

1982 Columbia completes first space shuttle flight.

1984 Two astronauts float in space as "human satellites."
• Kathryn Sullivan is the first American woman to walk in space.

| 1978 | 1979 | 1980 | 1981 | 1982 | 1983 | 1984 | 1985 |

1983 Sally Ride travels on space shuttle Challenger as first American woman in space.

Space

1986 Space shuttle Challenger explodes, killing all 7 astronauts including teacher Christa McAuliffe, the first private citizen in space.

1989 Unmanned spacecraft Galileo photographs the moon's far side.

1986	1987	1988	1989	1990	1991	1992

1988 Space shuttle Discovery relaunches space program.

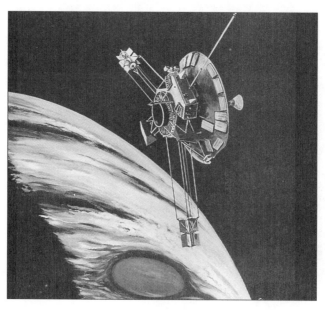

1992 Three astronauts leave their space shuttle to repair a damaged satellite 230 miles above Earth.

• Space shuttle Columbia travels 5,760,000 miles, circling Earth 221 times.

• After 14 years of service, unmanned spacecraft Pioneer 12 (*left*) has sent 400 billion pieces of information back to Earth.

Sports and Games

1585 English artist John White draws American Indian games— lacrosse, archery, foot racing.

1619 Virginia forbids playing dice or cards.

| 1580 • | 1610 • | • | 1620 • |

1621 Governor William Bradford is scandalized by ball playing in New Plymouth.

1611 Jamestown settlers bowl in the streets.

1651 Toys and dolls are sold in Boston shops.

1659 Governor Peter Stuyvesant forbids tennis playing on certain days.

1722 In New England, billiards is a popular recreation.

1650 • • • **1660** • **1720** •

1657 In New Amsterdam, settlers play *kolven*, an early form of golf.

1664 Horse racing, the first organized sport in the colonies, is popular in Virginia and New York. In Boston, colonists prefer football.

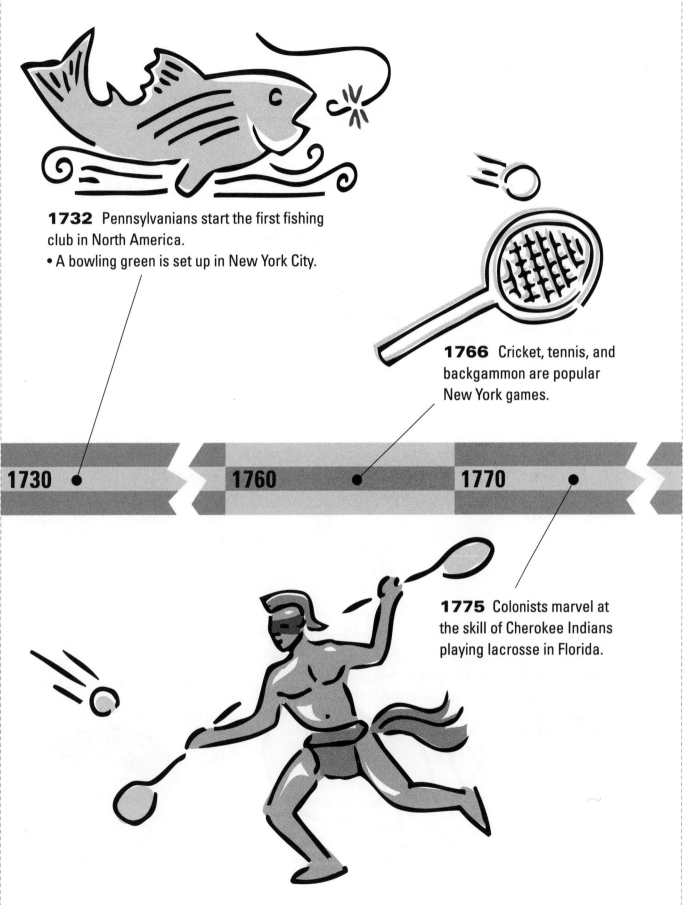

1732 Pennsylvanians start the first fishing club in North America.
• A bowling green is set up in New York City.

1766 Cricket, tennis, and backgammon are popular New York games.

1730 • 1760 • 1770 •

1775 Colonists marvel at the skill of Cherokee Indians playing lacrosse in Florida.

Sports and Games

1811 New York rowers defeat Long Island rowers in one of the first rowing races in the country.

1827 The first swimming school in the country opens in Boston. Beginning students are held up by a rope and pole!

1801 Log rolling and shooting contests are popular frontier recreations.

1820 College students begin playing soccer.

1825 Gymnastics is introduced to the United States from Germany.

1800 **1810** **1820**

1809 A cricket club is organized in Boston. The game is popular throughout the colonies.

1823 In the nation's first major horse race, the horse representing the North beat the horse of the South for a $20,000 prize.

1816 Jacob Hyer is America's first boxing champion.

1828 The nation's first archery club is formed.

1845 Alexander Cartwright, a New York fireman organizes the first baseball club, The Knickerbockers. Cartwright wrote rules for the game that are close to today's sport.

1851 The first baseball uniforms are white shirts, long blue trousers, and straw hats.
• Sailors for the United States win the America's Cup from England.

1833 An early form of baseball is played in Philadelphia.

1830 • **1840** • • • **1850** • •

1857 An American chess club is organized.

1844 A New York runner races 10 miles in less than an hour.

1846 The Knickerbockers lose to the New York Club in the first recorded baseball game in history.

Sports and Games

1863 An American inventor creates roller skates and the sport becomes popular overnight.
• A Philadelphia baseball player is the first recorded base stealer!

1875 The first Kentucky Derby is run.

1869 The first football game between college teams is played between Rutgers and Princeton.
• The first professional baseball team—the Cincinnati Red Stockings—is formed.

1878 The first bicycles are manufactured in the United States. Within four years there were 20,000 cyclists in the nation.

1860 Croquet is introduced from England.

| 1860 | • | • | • | • | 1870 | • | • | • | • | 1880 | • | • |

1861 Seneca runner Deerfoot outraces all of his competitors in a British race.

1874 Lawn tennis arrives in the United States from Bermuda.

1876 Polo is first played in the United States.
• Rules for the newly developed game of football—based on English rugby—were agreed upon.

1888 The Amateur Athletic Union is formed.

1867 The popularity of baseball explodes after the Civil War. The National Association of Base Ball Players has 237 teams.

1883 Yale wins the first national college football championship.

1894 Golf becomes more popular with 100 golf courses across the country.

1891 American gym teacher James Naismith invents the game of basketball.

1896 At the first modern Olympic Games the U.S. teams win 9 out of 12 events.

1900 The American League is formed in baseball.

1904 Organized automobile racing begins with the Vanderbilt Cup.
• The first Olympic Games held in the United States open in St. Louis.

1912 American Indian Jim Thorpe triumphs at the Olympic Games in Stockholm.

| 1890 ● | ● ● ● ● | 1900 ● ● | 1910 ● ● ● |

1895 The first professional football game is played in Pennsylvania.

1897 A New Yorker wins the first Boston Marathon in 2 hours, 55 minutes, 10 seconds

1903 After the National League is formed, the two baseball leagues compete in the first World Series.

1919 Jack Dempsey wins the world heavyweight boxing championship.

1893 Ice hockey is introduced from Canada.
• There are more than 1 million bicycles in the United States.

1911 The first Indianapolis 500 auto race is run.

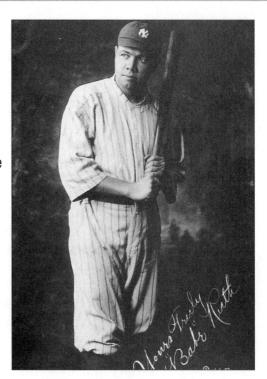

1927 Babe Ruth sets a home run record with 60 "homers" in the season (a record that will last until 1961).

1936 The Baseball Hall of Fame is established in Cooperstown, NY.

| 1920 | 1930 | 1940 |

1926 New Yorker Gertrude Ederle is the first woman to swim the English Channel.

1947 Jackie Robinson breaks the color barrier to become the first black player in baseball's major leagues.
• The first Little League World Series is played.

1950 The Minneapolis Lakers win the first NBA basketball championship.

1964 Muhammad Ali wins the world heavyweight boxing championship.

1974 Almost 34 million Americans played tennis this year.
• Evel Knievel jumps the Snake River Canyon on his motorcycle.
• Little League baseball is open to girls.

1960 Sixteen-year-old Bobby Fischer defends the U.S. chess championship.

1969 The first women jockeys ride in competition.

1950		1960		1970	

1957 The first U.S. runner breaks the four-minute mile.

1967 AFL and NFL football teams compete in the first Super Bowl.

1970 The first New York Marathon is run.

1962 Wilt Chamberlain is the first basketball player to score 100 points in a game.

1977 Brazilian soccer star Pelé helps soccer become the fastest growing team sport in the country.

Sports and Games

1986 The first American to sail nonstop around the world alone sets a new record—150 days.

1991 High schools report that more than a third of school athletes are women.
• There are 800 rodeos in the nation.
• Three American women finish in the top three places in the world figure skating championships—a world record.

1983 Baseball is America's favorite spectator sport; horse racing is second.

1980 • • •   **1990** • •

1984 A poll shows that fishing, bicycling, and swimming are Americans' favorite activities.

1990 Football sets records as America's favorite sport.

1996 Atlanta, Georgia, is the site of the 100th anniversary Olympic Games.

Getting the Vote

1639 Margaret Brent begins the woman suffrage movement when she demands suffrage—the right to vote—from the Maryland Assembly.
• America's first written constitution, the Fundamental Orders of Connecticut, says only freemen can vote.

1619 Virginia colonists vote in the House of Burgesses, the first representative government in the colonies.

1610	1620	1630

1631 Massachusetts colony says only men who are church members can vote.

1620 41 men sign the Mayflower Compact, agreeing to make laws for the Pilgrim colony.

1765 Colonists protest "taxation without representation" when Britain passes laws without allowing colonists to vote.

1777 Vermont is the first state to abolish slavery and allow all men to vote.

1640   1760   1770

1776 New Jersey passes the first colonial law giving women the vote. (They took away the right 31 years later.)
• Continental Congress votes to declare independence from Britain and become 13 united states.

1789 The new United States has a Constitution granting all white men the right to vote.
• George Washington is elected as nation's first President with 69 votes in the Electoral College. (At first, state legislatures voted for electors who voted for President; there was no popular vote.)

1848 At the Seneca Falls Convention women demand the right to vote.

1780   1800   1840

1800 States begin to allow voters (instead of state legislatures) to choose presidential electors.

1804 The Twelfth Amendment to the Constitution allows electors to vote for President and Vice President separately.

1870 The Fifteenth Amendment says no state can take away a citizen's right to vote regardless of race, color, or previous condition of servitude.

1878 Women's suffrage amendment introduced and defeated in Congress (which would happen each year until 1920).

1856 North Carolina is last state to end requirement that voters be property owners.

1868 Suffragette Susan B. Anthony founds suffrage newspaper *The Revolution*.

1850	•	1860	•	•	1870	•	•

1869 Elizabeth Cady Stanton and Susan B. Anthony found National Woman Suffrage Association.
• Wyoming Territory is first in nation to give women the right to vote.

1860 African Americans can vote in 6 of the 34 states.

1872 Susan B. Anthony is arrested and fined $100 for leading women to vote in presidential election.

1890 Mississippi's state constitution uses literacy requirements to keep African Americans from voting.

1918 President Wilson supports woman suffrage, but Congress says no.

1884 National Equal Rights Party nominates Belva Lockwood as first woman candidate for President.

1899 Voting machines first used in elections.

1880	1890	1910

1888 Secret ballots first used in elections.

1913 The Seventeenth Amendment allows the people to vote directly for U. S. senators (before this, state legislatures chose senators).

1917 Suffragists picket the White House.

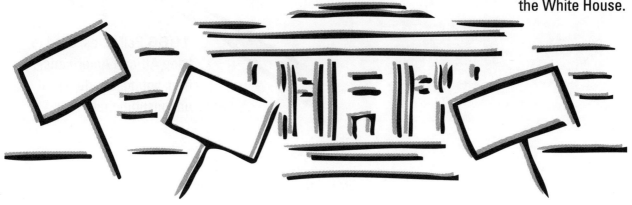

1920 The Nineteenth Amendment grants women the right to vote.

1965 President Johnson requests sweeping changes in voting laws to protect African Americans' right to vote.
• Civil rights protests call for voter registration.

1920 1950 1960

1957 U.S. government supervises voting to protect African Americans' right to vote.

1966 Poll taxes, used to keep African Americans from voting, are declared unconstitutional.

1975 All literacy requirements for voting are ended.

1992 There are 129 million registered voters in the U.S.

1970 ● ●

1990 ●

1971 The 26th Amendment lowers voting age from 21 to 18.

Kids in History

1007 Snorro, the first European child born in North America, is born to Viking parents.

| 1000 |

| 1490 |

| 1580 |

1492 10 "gromets," cabin boys, voyage to the Americas with Christopher Columbus.

1587 Virginia Dare is born in Virginia, the first English child born in North America.

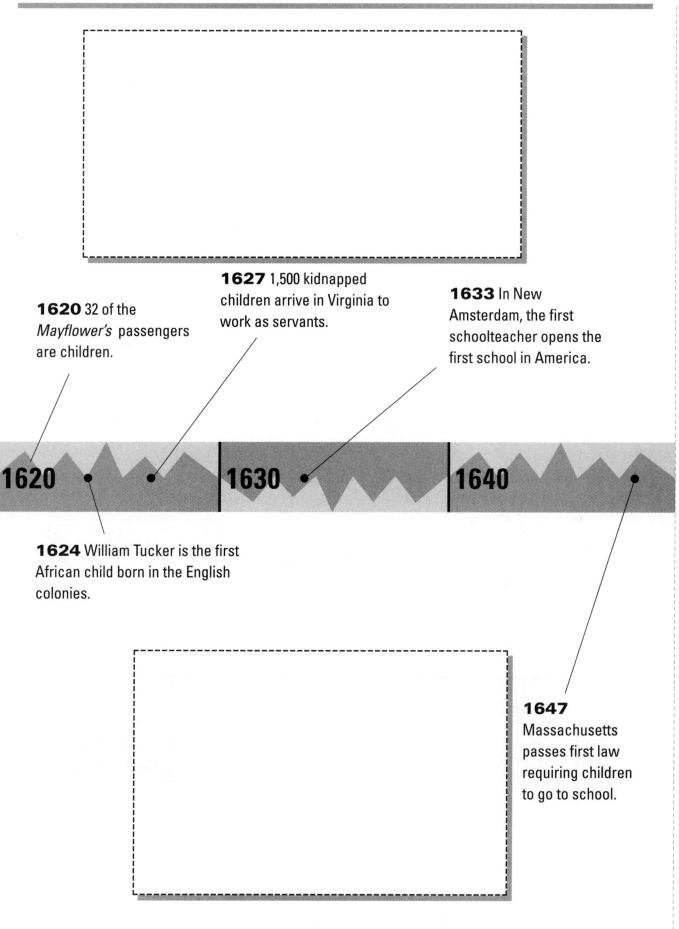

1620 32 of the *Mayflower's* passengers are children.

1627 1,500 kidnapped children arrive in Virginia to work as servants.

1633 In New Amsterdam, the first schoolteacher opens the first school in America.

1620

1630

1640

1624 William Tucker is the first African child born in the English colonies.

1647 Massachusetts passes first law requiring children to go to school.

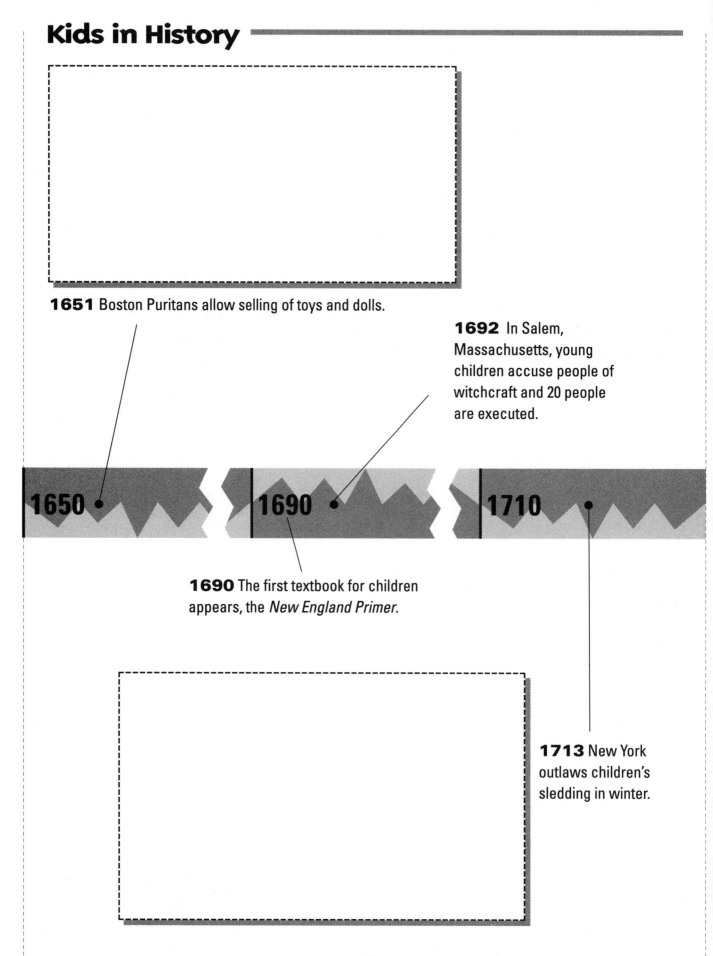

1651 Boston Puritans allow selling of toys and dolls.

1692 In Salem, Massachusetts, young children accuse people of witchcraft and 20 people are executed.

1650

1690

1710

1690 The first textbook for children appears, the *New England Primer*.

1713 New York outlaws children's sledding in winter.

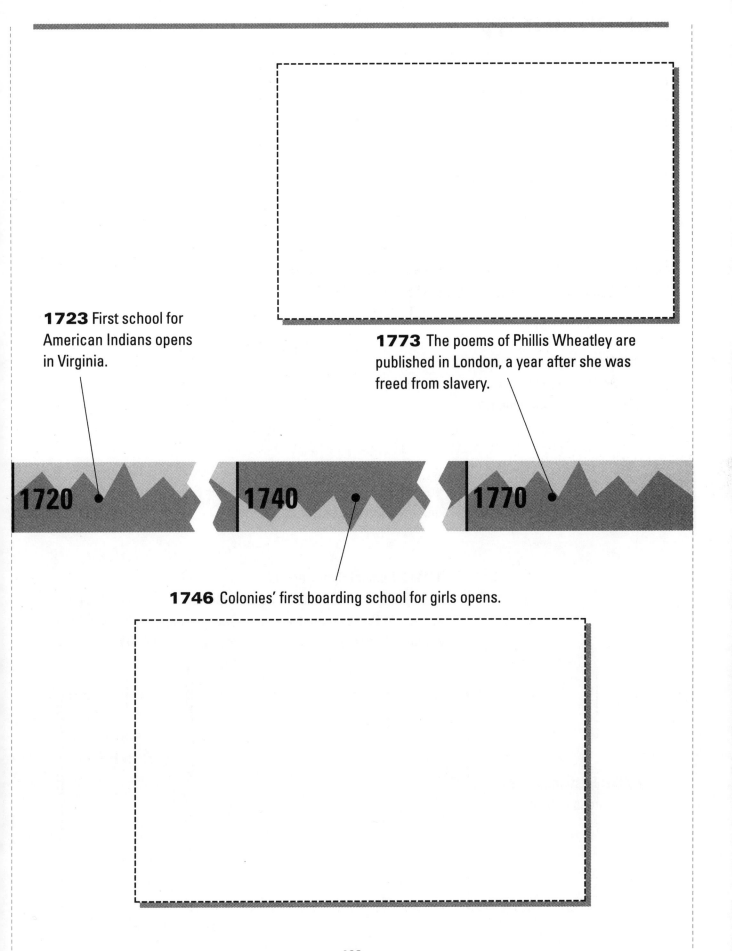

1723 First school for American Indians opens in Virginia.

1773 The poems of Phillis Wheatley are published in London, a year after she was freed from slavery.

1720

1740

1770

1746 Colonies' first boarding school for girls opens.

Kids in History

1798 The first model train is built.

1787 Colonial author argues that women must be educated so that they can educate their children.

1780

1790

1800

1790 Samuel Slater opens Rhode Island cotton mill using secrets of British industry and workers 4-10 years old.

1805 A baby boy is born to Sacajawea, Shoshone guide to the Lewis and Clark expedition.

1789 First children's magazine is published.

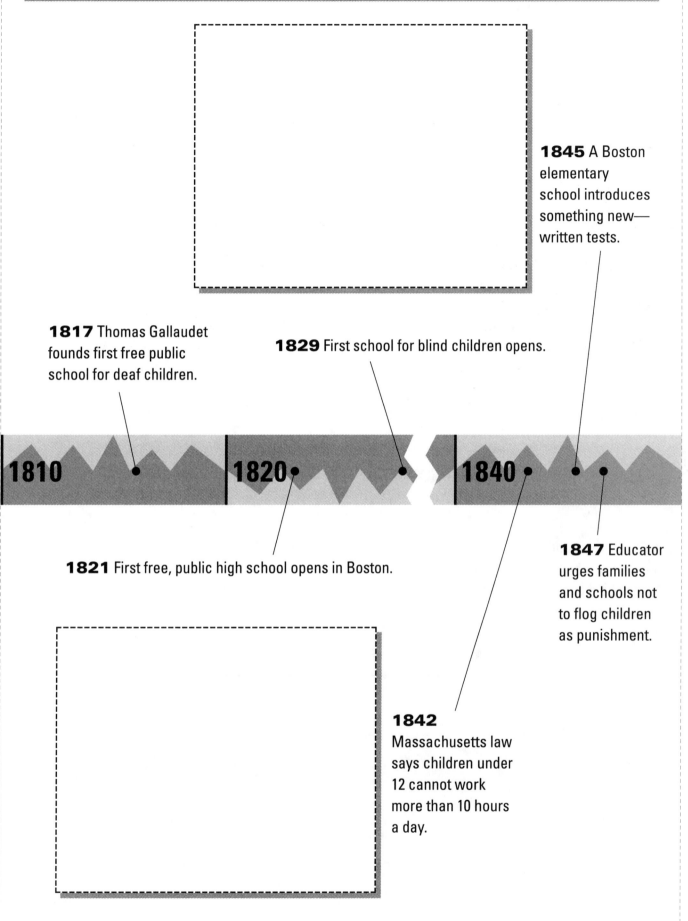

1845 A Boston elementary school introduces something new— written tests.

1817 Thomas Gallaudet founds first free public school for deaf children.

1829 First school for blind children opens.

1810

1820

1840

1821 First free, public high school opens in Boston.

1847 Educator urges families and schools not to flog children as punishment.

1842 Massachusetts law says children under 12 cannot work more than 10 hours a day.

Kids in History

1878 The first bicycles are manufactured in the United States.

1851 The Asylum for Friendless Boys is founded in New York as a home for juvenile delinquents and abused children.

1856 The nation's first kindergarten opens in Wisconsin. • Children's Day is first celebrated in American churches.

1863 Roller skates are invented.

1874 Law says children cannot work more than 10 hours a day in a factory.

1850   1860   1870

1852 Massachusetts requires all children 8 to 14 years old to attend school at least 12 weeks a year.

1861 First summer camp for boys opens.

1870 Census counts 750,000 child laborers under the age of 15.

1875 The Society for the Prevention of Cruelty to Children is organized.

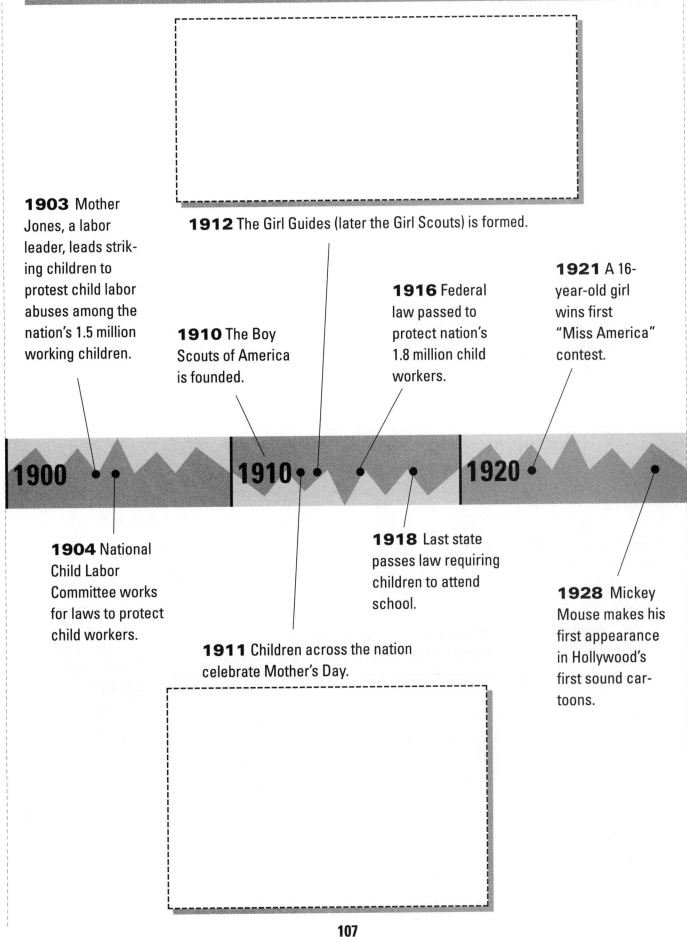

1903 Mother Jones, a labor leader, leads striking children to protest child labor abuses among the nation's 1.5 million working children.

1912 The Girl Guides (later the Girl Scouts) is formed.

1921 A 16-year-old girl wins first "Miss America" contest.

1916 Federal law passed to protect nation's 1.8 million child workers.

1910 The Boy Scouts of America is founded.

1900

1910

1920

1904 National Child Labor Committee works for laws to protect child workers.

1918 Last state passes law requiring children to attend school.

1928 Mickey Mouse makes his first appearance in Hollywood's first sound cartoons.

1911 Children across the nation celebrate Mother's Day.

Kids in History

1955 Report states that 1 billion comic books are sold in the U.S. each year.

1951 Linda Brown's father begins lawsuit that will lead to desegregation of public schools in 1954.

1936 Shirley Temple, 8 years old, is top Hollywood star.

1947 Little League baseball starts a world series.

1930　　**1940**　　**1950**

1954 Schoolchildren first vaccinated against polio.

1949 Smart kids star in Quiz Kids television show.

1957 Nine African American students integrate Little Rock, Arkansas, high school.

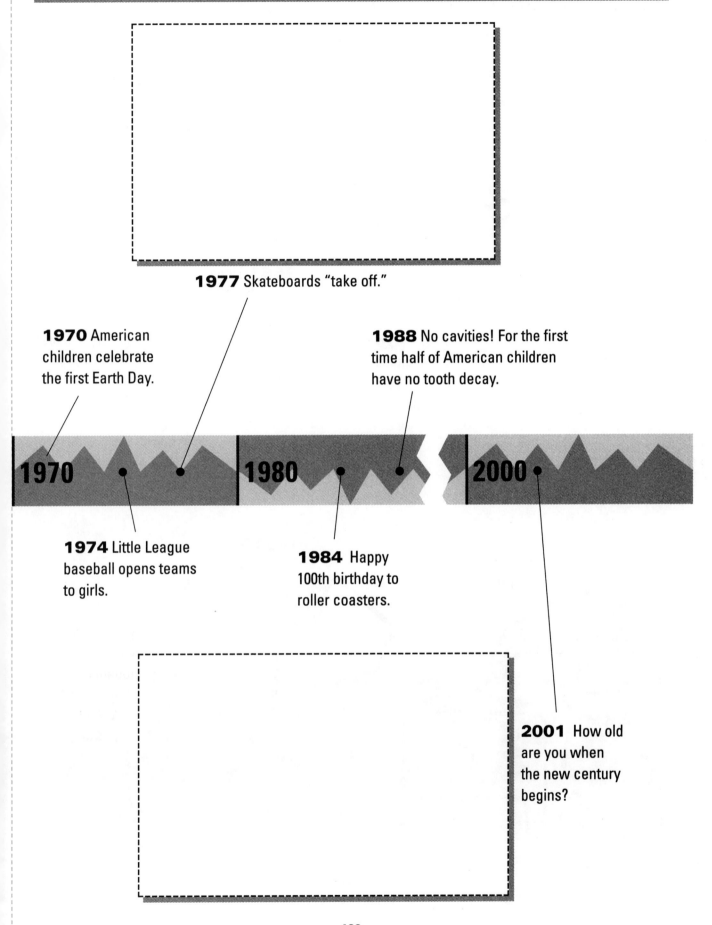

1977 Skateboards "take off."

1970 American children celebrate the first Earth Day.

1988 No cavities! For the first time half of American children have no tooth decay.

1970

1980

2000

1974 Little League baseball opens teams to girls.

1984 Happy 100th birthday to roller coasters.

2001 How old are you when the new century begins?

Ben Franklin

1706 Born in Boston, the 15th of 17 children.

1723 Runs away to Philadelphia, the largest city in the colonies. In 7 years he will own his own print shop.

1737 Becomes Philadelphia's postmaster. He will set up the first city mail delivery and first public library.

1700 •	1710 •	1720 •	1730 • •	1740 •

1718 Apprenticed to his brother James, a printer.

1733 First publishes *Poor Richard's Almanac*, filled with wise sayings.

1744 Invents the Franklin Stove to save fuel.

1752 Using a kite, shows that lightning is electricity.

1776 Helps write the Declaration of Independence.

1757 Represents the colonies in London, where he helps repeal the Stamp Act.

1783 Signs the treaty ending the Revolution.

1790 Dies at age 84.

1750 • •	1760	1770 •	1780 • • •	1790

1754 Invents bifocal eyeglasses.
• Presents a plan to unite the 13 colonies.

1788 Becomes president of the first American antislavery society, urging the abolition of slavery.

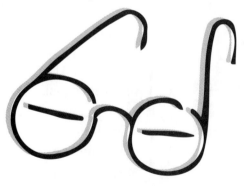

1787 Guides the new nation in writing the Constitution. He is the oldest delegate at the convention.

Harriet Tubman

1830s Works as a field hand, plowing and hauling wood.

1821 Probably born in this year, in Maryland, to enslaved parents Benjamin Ross and Harriet Greene.

1820	1830	1840

1844 Marries John Tubman, a free black.

1849 Escapes from slavery and goes north to Philadelphia, guided by the North Star. Soon begins her work as a "conductor" on the Underground Railroad.

1861 Works for the Union army as a nurse, scout, and spy. In one campaign she rescues more than 750 African Americans.

1869 *Scenes from the Life of Harriet Tubman* is published. Earnings are used to help elderly and poor African Americans.

1857 Rescues her parents from slavery. Tubman was called Moses, because she led about 300 enslaved people to freedom.

| 1850 | 1860 | 1870 | 1910 |

1913 Dies on March 10.

1860 Becomes active in the fight for women's rights.

Thomas Edison

1857 Taught at home by his mother because he was "slow" in school. He loved chemistry but was bad in math.

1879 Makes the first practical electric lights.

1847 Born February 11 in Milan, Ohio.

1870 Starts his "invention factory," employing 50 people.

1840	1850	1860	1870

1863 Becomes a telegraph operator after working on the railroad. Begins inventing labor-saving devices for the telegraph.

1869 Registers his first patents—for a vote recorder and a stock ticker.

1877 Produces the first phonograph, which he later calls his favorite invention.

1882 Sets up power plant in New York that is the first central power station to supply electricity to a large area.

1928 Awarded a gold medal by U.S. Congress "for developoment and application of inventions that have revolutionized civilization."

| 1880 • | 1890 • | 1920 | 1930 • |

1931 Dies at age 84, after patenting 1,093 inventions in his lifetime.

1891 Contributes to the development of motion pictures.

Eleanor Roosevelt

1918 Becomes active in the Red Cross when U.S. enters World War I.

1899 Sent to "finishing school" in England for four years.

1928 Becomes First Lady of NY state when FDR is elected governor.

1906 Daughter Anna is born, the first of six children.

1884 Born to a wealthy family, niece of President Theodore Roosevelt.

| 1880 | 1890 | 1900 | 1910 | 1920 |

1894 Orphaned after the death of both parents within two years.

1905 Marries her distant cousin, Franklin Delano Roosevelt.

1910 Franklin begins his political career with election as NY state senator.

1921 Takes on active role in FDR's career when he is stricken with polio.

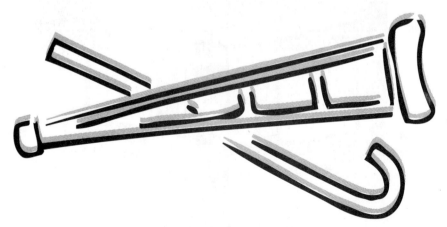

1958 Gallup Poll shows that she is the nation's most admired woman.

1932 Becomes First Lady of the U.S. when FDR is elected to first of four terms as President.

1945 FDR dies in office.
• Appointed by President Truman as one of five delegates to first United Nations General Assembly in London.

1961 Appointed by President Kennedy to U.S. delegation to the UN.

1937 Writes autobiography, *This Is My Story*.

| 1930 • • • | 1940 • • • | 1950 • | 1960 • • |

1935 Daily newspaper column "My Day" begins publication in more than 60 papers.

1948 Addresses UN General Assembly in Paris.

1962 Dies in New York at age 77.

1946 Writes *This I Remember* about FDR's presidency.

Martin Luther King, Jr.

1929 Born in Atlanta on January 15, son of a Baptist minister.

1944 Graduates from high school and enters Morehouse College at age 15.

1920	1930	1940

1934 By the age of 5, knows Bible passages and hymns by heart.

1947 Ordained as a minister.

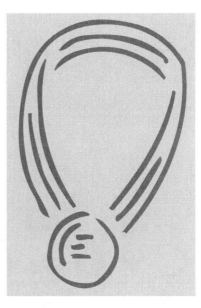

1964 Awarded Nobel Peace Prize for civil right efforts. At 35 was youngest ever awarded the prize.

1951 Graduates from Crozer Theological Seminary at the top of his class. Has become a follower of Gandhi.

1957 Becomes head of Southern Christian Leadership Conference, which he has founded with 115 other black leaders.

1965 Leads voting right march from Selma to Montgomery, Alabama.

1950 • • • •	1960 • • • •

1955 Receives Ph.D. from Boston University.
• Comes to national attention as leader of Montgomery, Alabama, bus boycott.

1958 *Stride Toward Freedom* is published.

1963 Writes "Letter from Birmingham Jail" while jailed after leading civil rights protests.
• Tells crowd of 250,000 at Lincoln Memorial "I Have a Dream."

1968 Assassinated on April 4 in Memphis, Tennessee.